MOTHER'S MANTRAS

As Spoken By

Susie W. Jefferson

Thank you, Momma,

for indelibly imprinting

your words along our spines.

Mother's Mantras

As Spoken By

Susie W. Jefferson

Presented By

George C. Jefferson Jr.
Dr. Latonia J. Lewis
Dr. Mary M. Jefferson
Latisha A. Jefferson
and **Richette P. Hudson**

Cover Design By

Sun Child Wind Spirit

Proofread By

Latisha A. Jefferson

Edited By

Mylia Tiye Mal Jaza

Mother's Mantras

First Edition. Printed In the USA.
Recycled Paper Encouraged.

ISBN-10: 1541177533
ISBN-13: 978-1-5411-7753-6

Authors

Susie W. Jefferson
GoddessMother@bepublished.biz
www.bepublished.biz

Mylia Tiye Mal Jaza
GoddessSage@bepublished.biz
www.bepublished.org

Self-Publishing Associate
Dr. Mary M. Jefferson
BePublished.Org
(972) 880-8316
70 W. Madison, #1400
Chicago, IL 60602
P.O. Box 8324
Jackson, MS 39284
mari@bepublished.org

Imprint of Record
CreateSpace On-Demand Publishing
7290-B Investment Drive
Charleston, SC 29418

Table of Content

Mother's Business Mantras

"Don't ignore bad news, bill collectors, or letters you get from anybody. Take the time to read and understand everything in front of you, especially if it's something legal. Don't ever sign nothing from nobody without reading it for yourself, even if they say they're telling you what the papers say."

"Keep you a nice dress, a pair of stockings, a coat, a receipt book, and some unscuffed shoes in your trunk in case you get a last-minute invitation to appear somewhere to speak, host or sing."

"Don't spend every penny you get. Always pay your tithes and offerings, put up money into savings, and stick to your budget."

"If you get something on credit, pay it back and pay it off as soon as possible to cut down on interest. Honestly, it's best to just avoid getting anything if you don't have the cash to pay for it in full right then."

"If you're not going to do it right, leave it alone instead of half-doing it!"

"Always put God first, and there is nothing you cannot do and do well."

"When people at work start gossiping, stay away and quiet."

"Never be arrogant or too proud, and never think you are better than or beneath anybody."

"Enunciate your words but don't over-pronounce a word, and don't break a verb."

"Slow your cadence. Stop talking so fast. Give people more than a couple of seconds to start responding to you. Not everybody's brain works at the speed of yours. Be quiet and listen a while longer and you'll be amazed at the conversations you can have with people, what you can learn, and how much they will enjoy talking to you."

Mother's Family Mantras

"Okay, let's hold hands and say grace. But from now on when it's your turn to quote a scripture, nobody better not ever say, 'Jesus wept' again."

"You all are siblings, and you should love each other better. When I'm gone, all y'all will have to count on is one another."

"I don't allow no fighting, and you and your sisters and brother better not be arguing."

"What did you say? Well, if you didn't say nothing you must have thought it 'cause I sure heard it!"

"Playtime is over. I need to see your head in a book."

"Ain't no Fs coming in this house! Anything less than a B means this belt, your ass, and no more going to games or staying after school for extra-curricular activities. You coming up out of everything until those grades get back up and stay there."

"If you can't find something of yours, don't blame nobody for it. You look for it! And, look everywhere three times before you even fix your mind to start conceiving blaming somebody."

"Let another teacher call me, and I will come to that school and beat your ass in front of that whole class like you stole something! Bet you won't act up again!"

"Ain't no babies coming up in this house! You're grown enough to get pregnant, you're grown enough to get out. Two grown women can't live in the same house."

"You wanna runaway, runaway. But I recommend you already have a place to stay and some income otherwise you'll becoming right back here or be out there being mistreated. Because, ain't nobody gone let you stay with them for free except your mother with rules – and that's where you say you don't wanna be. Ha,ha,ha. Welcome back, that was quick. See. What I tell you? Ha,ha,ha. We'll just say you took a walk to think. Now, go wash your hands. We're about to eat."

"Ump. Well, I'll just talk to you another time. I'm about to hang up in your face and go to sleep. Goodnight. Have a sweet dream, baby. I love you to death."

"This house ain't clean! Y'all hadn't done nothing since I've been gone! I shouldn't have to tell y'all to clean up! Why you wanna live in filth? Pick up behind yourselves. If you use it, wash it. If you break it, fix it or throw it away if it can't be fixed. If you see it on the floor and it shouldn't be there, pick it up and don't step over it. When you're sweeping and mopping, hit the corners too and clean under every piece of furniture that broom and mop can get under. Don't forget to dust, and do the ceiling fan too. And, if you go to sleep with dirty dishes in the sink, you gone wake up to me whipping your ass all the way back to the kitchen sink."

"Why you keep coming home with these girls that already got babies? I know didn't no child ask to come here and somebody gotta help raise 'em, but it ain't gotta be you."

"Say or do what you want to me! I don't allow nobody to put their mouth and hands on my children!"

"I may not look good or have the best, but I make sure my children do."

"I'm tired of whipping you and ain't no more punishments left. I'll just whip you for this tomorrow when you do something else. I know your pattern now, and you ain't gone ride my last nerve to death."

"Don't have nobody in my house when I'm not here."

Mother's Life Mantras

"Be good to yourself and the people around you. Always treat people the way you want to be treated."

"Always keep up your hygiene and good grooming, and always dress properly for the occasion."

"Don't let your parents down, they brought you up."

"Be a master of your habits, or they will master you."

"Guard your thoughts; What you think, you are."

"See what you can do for others, not what they can do for you."

"Treasure your time. Don't spend it. Invest it."

"Stand for something positive, or you will fall for anything."

"Don't fill upon this world's crumbs. Feed your soul on the living bread."

"Give your all to Christ, He gave His all for you."

"Go straight to the store in my car. Don't make no stops and don't give nobody no damn ride."

"Let the wind wake 'em up!"

"Don't speed up. Let them fly right on past you. There's something waiting down the road."

"Laughing is catching. You laugh at a distasteful joke, you're in agreement with it. You laugh at someone's bad condition, you're gonna end up in that same position."

"I don't know who you think you are, but I know FOR A FACT you don't know me. You need to crank that down some decibels if your life insurance isn't paid up."

"What the hell you say? You don't know I got your burial paid up!"

"People can take your joy, money, friends and family from you: But, the one thing nobody can EVER take from you is knowledge! Get all the education you can from these schools and every person you meet in this life. Even the homeless people on drugs we serve food to can teach us to be better reflection of God. Never stop learning."

"I don't even wanna hear you breathe."

"I brought you into this world. Child, don't think I won't take you out."

"Come here. I'm gone give you something to cry about. Ain't no use in crying for nothing, wasting tears."

"This hurts me just as much as this whipping is gone hurt you."

"Did you try to help him? If you didn't offer to help, why do you think it's cute to be making fun of him? Don't you ever fix your mouth to say nothing about what somebody is going through if you haven't tried to help that person. And, don't ever make fun of nobody because of what they don't have. That same person has something else that's better than what you have. How would you like for him to go around making fun of you?"

Mother's Love Mantras

"Select only a date who will make a good mate."

"Whoever loves you, treat them right. If somebody is abusing you, defend yourself and leave them alone. Never stay with or go back to a person who mistreats you or it will get worse."

"This crazy stuff y'all going through, I'm so glad I ain't never been in love."

"When the right one for you comes along, you won't have to deal with all that foolishness or carry nobody else's weight."

"Don't accept no wooden nickels, and don't put up with no 'anythang' just to have somebody around you."

"Don't get married just to get out of the house or for any reason other than a love you can trust."

"Don't you marry nobody you already know brings you the kind of problems you are not willing to go through forever, unless you just want to be miserable and end up divorced. Marriage is not required for adulthood."

"If you get married and you all are planning to divorce, be sure you all cannot work things out before you go file. But, make sure you file first. That way, you can avoid having to waste money fighting against a whole lot of lies just to get your divorce and live in peace."

"As long as you love yourself, you can always be loved and show love. Take care of yourself, and be kind to everybody you meet. You never know, that smile of yours might be the only good thing somebody was shown that day."

"I love you and always will."

Mother's Social Mantras

"Watch the company you keep. Never be a follower. If anything, be that positive example."

"Choose your companions with care. You may become what they are."

"If you kept that a secret, don't go trying to tell it now because you're mad and want them to get in trouble. You're in trouble too, because you got in on it when you agreed to keep silent."

"Your reputation precedes you."

"I know what you and your friends have been doing, and every spot y'all went to tonight. Don't ever think you can do something in secret. There are always eyes on you! And when you swear up and down nobody sees you, rest assured at least three people are watching your every move and taking note."

"That girl is not your friend. She secretly envies and despises you. I saw the way she cut her eyes at you when you turned your back to her. Your best bet is to take her back and leave her where you found her, and don't associate with her again. You don't believe me? Keep on hanging around her and you'll see."

"If you tell somebody, 'No,' and they still keep asking, tell 'em 'Hell no,' and change the conversation or walk away."

"Don't tell somebody you're gonna do something and then you just throw something together or don't even try to keep your word. There is no honor in misleading people and it is not right to have people expecting something you know full well you are not going to give them. And, you make sure you don't expect no more from anybody than what you know you are willing to give and what you've already seen them do, or you'll be setting yourself up for disappointment too."

THE ART & ARTISTS

THE BOOK

Published with the assistance of BePublished.Org, **Mother's Mantras** is Mylia Tiye Mal Jaza's 17th published guerilla-glue release and the first American book release solely comprised of words as told by Goddess Mother **Susie W. Jefferson** (a native of Hazlehurst and longtime Jackson resident).

A book comprised of some of the plethora nuggets of wisdom her exemplary mother shared with all five of her children, Jaza hopes the timeless advice will help not only parents, but people in general who want the best life possible no matter what position into which they find themselves thrust.

Page after page is filled with familiar quotes and new ones to every reader. Not everyone will agree with every quote. Yet, no reader will put this book down without obtaining some new lesson, perspective, reminder, chuckle, motivation or shock.

The willingness of Goddess Mother Jefferson's children to "share Momma" with people who need such a matriarch will benefit families owning **Mother's Mantras** for many lifetimes. Because of this, Jaza considers this work her most-prized book of all.

THE SPEAKER/AUTHOR

Susie W. Jefferson is the fifth of seven children, the mother of five, grandmother of ten, great-grandmother of four, and godmother to scores. A Mississippi native raised in Hazlehurst who relocated to Jackson more than 30 years ago, the mother knows first-hand the challenges spouses and single parents face when trying to provide for, protect, and guide children through life.

Goddess Mother Jefferson had long dreamed of becoming an author, and had begun writing her autobiography years ago. With the compilation of her words by her children to create and release **Mother's Mantras**, the beloved philanthropist's dream of becoming an author finally came true for Christmas in 2016.

"Sue" has already been renowned throughout Central Mississippi for her culinary arts and events planning skills for more than 50 years. An honor roll student awarded "Most Coachable Player" in Track & Field for being the team's fastest runner and participating in all the relays and long-distance runs, she attended Parrish High School in Hazlehurst.

After completing high school, the Goddess Mother worked at places including Royal Maid and the Copiah County Health Department before retiring early due to nearly dying from aneurysms. And, although she continues to battle Myasthenia Gravitz as well as other illnesses to date, Goddess Mother Jefferson maintains her faith in God, love and support of family, sense of humor, diligent spirit, devotion to fellowship, and outreach to those in need.

GoddessMother@BePublished.biz

THE PROOFREADER

Latisha A. Jefferson (author of The Artistic Sketch of Me published in 2008) is **Susie W. Jefferson**'s fourth child who made her editorial debut by providing proofreading services as a member of the BePublished.Org team releasing **Mother's Mantras** by Mylia Tiye Mal Jaza in December 2016. When Jefferson's own book was released, it was Jaza assigned to provide the poet with editing services as a part of the BePublished.Org editorial team in Autumn 2008.

An award-winning poet whose first celebrated seeing some of her poetry published in 2003 in Jaza's second book of a dual series (Life Is Beautiful: La Vita Es Hermosa), the Mississippi resident and former Carnegie Hall singer enjoys socializing and indulging in movies, music, dominos, cards and cartoons. Jefferson also enjoys dancing and reading, and she is gifted with a loving heart that is unconditional for all – especially children and those with special needs. Her upcoming projects include completing a children's book and a second book of poetry.

BabytJjefferson@yahoo.com

THE AUTHOR/EDITOR

Mylia Tiye Mal Jaza (Mary "Mari" Michelle Jefferson) is **Susie W. Jefferson**'s third of five children. She is a former Texas resident and Mississippi native presently residing in Illinois. Jaza graduated from Jackson State University and the University of Texas at Dallas, and holds an honorary doctorate degree from Trinity Evangelical Christian University.

The entrepreneur, former professional model, and wedding officiant is also an award-winning journalist who gives back to the communities in which she lives and conducts business by mentoring teens, cleaning highways, feeding the homeless, providing gifts to nursing home residents, organizing community art exhibits and music festivals, and conducting school supplies drives for youth.

Also known as Sun Child Wind Spirit, Jaza (aka Goddess Sage) is a vocalist who has performed alongside international artists and at popular venues. She also helps writers with an array of editorial and business services including self-publishing and promotions training through BePublished.Org.

Prior to the December 2016 release of **Mother's Mantras**, two of Mylia's 16 published books were works she republished that were written by ancestors of hers – The Facts Of Reconstruction by John R. Lynch and The Old Negro And The New Negro by T. Leroy Jefferson, M.D. In addition to **Mother's Mantras**, Mylia's other 14 books were original works she created that ranged in content from poetry and prose to film and television scripts:

Life Is Beautiful: La Vita E Bella, Life Is Beautiful: La Vita Es Hermosa, Seen In Other Words, Plea For Peace, All For Show, Scientific Evidence God Exists, Elegies Of A Goddess, AND, Get Off Your Packages, My Plan For Every Bully, Stop & Tie Your Shoes, P.E.N.I.S., When The Quarterback Got Cut, and FOOLISH OF ME: Addressing Love Unappreciated.

MaryJefferson.us
BePublished.biz

MarryUsNow.us
BePublished.org

Order Books By Mylia Jaza & Family

Thank you for your support.

Life Is Beautiful:
La Vita E Bella
$20/soft x ______

The Old Negro And The New Negro
by T. Leroy Jefferson M.D.
______ x $20/soft
______ x $35/hard

Life Is Beautiful:
La Vita Es Hermosa
$15/soft x ______

All For Show:
Film & Television Scripts
______ x $25/soft

Seen In Other Words
$10/soft x ______

Plea For Peace
______ x $10/soft

The Facts Of Reconstruction
by John R. Lynch
$25/soft x ______

Scientific Evidence
God Exists
______ x $15/soft
______ x $30/hard

AND
$15/soft x ______

Elegies Of A Goddess
______ x $15/soft

READER ____

ADDRESS ______________________________ **UNIT #** ________

CITY ____________________________ **ST** _______ **ZIP** __________

EMAIL ____________________ **COUNTY** ___________ **COUNTRY** ______

Remit Payment For Selected Books + Form + $5 s/h To:

Mary M. Jefferson
P.O. Box 8324
Jackson, MS 39284

Please allow three (3) weeks minimum delivery to allow for order processing, autographing of books, and shipment to your address provided above.

Which Book(s) Autographed Using Which Individual(s) Name(s):

Your Thoughts About Recipient(s):

Personal Message From You To Author(s):

Other Books By Mylia Jaza & Family

Thank you for your support.

Children's Book
The Animals by Isaiah Walls Palmer
$25/soft x ______

Cat's Colors by Kelvin T. Johnson
Children's Book
______ x $25/soft

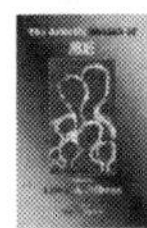

The Artistic Sketch Of Me
by Latisha A. Jefferson
$20/soft x ______

My Plan For Every Bully
Children's Book
______ x $25/soft

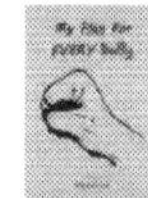

Stop And Tie Your Shoes
by Latisha A. Jefferson
$20/soft x ______

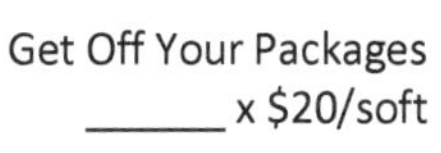

Get Off Your Packages
______ x $20/soft

P.E.N.I.S.
$20/soft x ______

When The Quarterback Got Cut
______ x $20/soft

Foolish of Me:
Addressing Love Unappreciated
______ x $20/soft

READER ______________________________

ADDRESS ______________________ **UNIT #** ________

CITY ____________________ **ST** ______ **ZIP** ________

EMAIL ________________ **COUNTY** __________ **COUNTRY** ______

<u>Remit Payment For Selected Books + Form + $5 s/h To:</u>

Mary M. Jefferson
P.O. Box 8324
Jackson, MS 39284

Please allow three (3) weeks minimum delivery to allow for order processing, autographing of books, and shipment to your address provided to us above.

Which Book(s) Autographed Using Which Individual(s) Name(s):

____

____

____

____

Your Thoughts About Recipient(s):

____

____

____

____

Personal Message From You To Author(s):

____

____

____

____

____

____

____

Made in the USA
Columbia, SC
31 March 2024